COZY CHRISTMAS
CUTE & SIMPLE COLORING BOOK

Cute and Cozy Coloring Book
for Adults & Teens Featuring Easy
and Bold Christmas Designs

COLORING BOOK
Cafe

www.coloringbookcafe.com

CONNECT WITH US

(@coloringbookcafe)

THIS BOOK BELONGS TO

_____

_____

MINDFUL COLORING

In an era where the pace of life seems to quicken by the day, nurturing our mental well-being has never been more crucial. At Coloring Book Cafe, we understand the power of artistic immersion in revitalizing the spirit. Our collection isn't just about coloring—it's a journey of self-discovery, a palette of joy, and a sanctuary of inner peace amidst life's hustle and bustle.

PAPER QUALITY

Our carefully selected standard quality paper ensures affordability without compromising on your coloring experience. Worried about bleeding with certain pens and markers? Simply slip a thicker sheet of paper behind your masterpiece to prevent any mishaps. Thank you for choosing Coloring Book Cafe, where creativity meets convenience!

SHARE YOUR MASTERPIECES

Join our community of inspired colorists who turn pages into living art. Share your colorful journey with us through reviews, photos, and videos, and let your creativity shine bright. We can't wait to marvel at your one-of-a-kind masterpieces!

Find the digital version of this title & many more digital releases on:

www.digitalbookcafe.com

Have questions? Let us know.
support@coloringbookcafe.com

30+ FREE DIGITAL COLORING PAGES

Thank you for choosing Coloring Book Cafe!
Visit **www.coloringbookcafe.com** and click on our link to download your **FREE** digital coloring pages

SHARE YOUR ARTWORK WITH US

(@coloringbookcafe)

BEFORE EMBARKING ON YOUR COLORING JOURNEY,
WARM UP YOUR IMAGINATION WITH
OUR CURATED THUMBNAILS >>

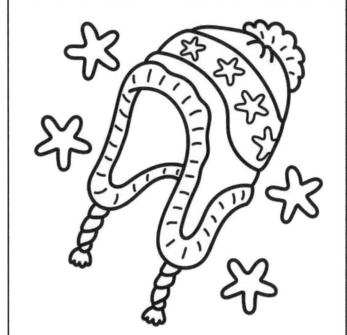

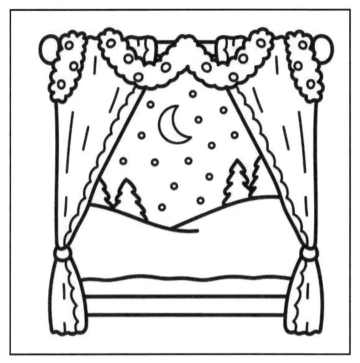

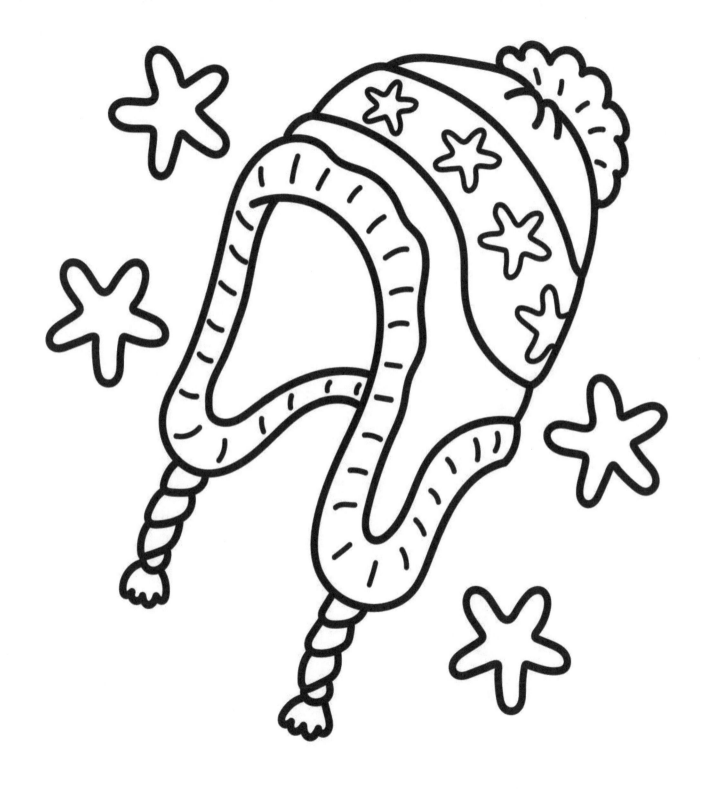

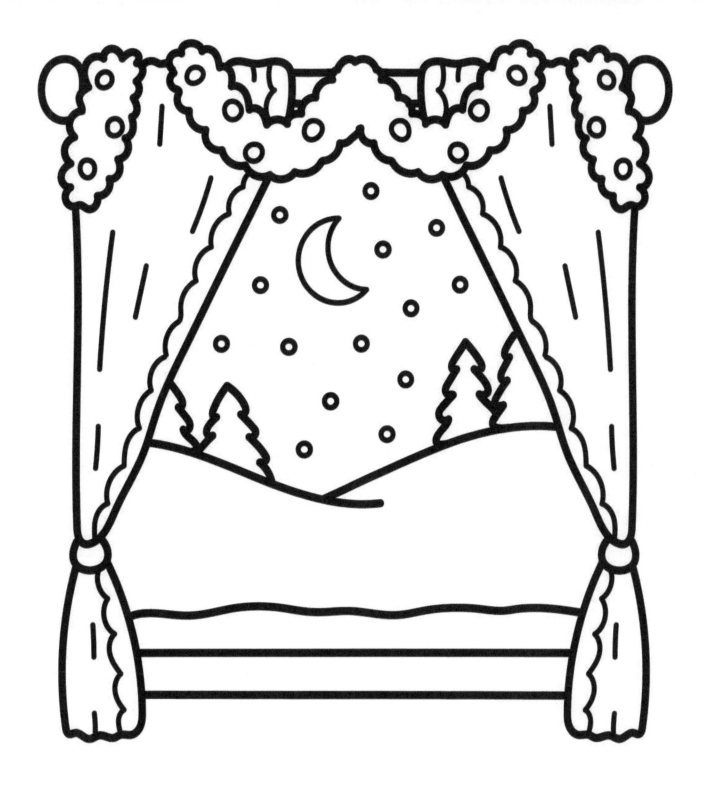

COLOR CHART

COLORING BOOK
Cafe

Thank You
For Your Purchase

We at Coloring Book Cafe are commited to deliver the best coloring illustrations to our community and we thank you for your support.

Please visit our digital store at:
www.digitalbookcafe.com

Claim your **FREE DIGITAL BOOK** at:
www.freecoloringbooklet.com

Find us on **INSTAGRAM**:
instagram.com/coloringbookcafe

Find us on **FACEBOOK**:
facebook.com/coloringbookcafe

Find us on **AMAZON**:
Search for "Coloring Book Cafe" and find our complete paperback collection on our Amazon Stores in CANADA, USA, AUSTRALIA & The UK

Made in United States
Troutdale, OR
10/29/2024

24268082R00064